Transportation Around the World

Trains

Chris Oxlade

Heinemann Library
Chicago, Illinois

Customer Service 888-454-2279
Visit our website at www.heinemannraintree.com

Designed by Kimberly R. Miracle, Ray Hendren, Cavedweller Studio and Q2A Creative
Printed in China by South China Printing Company

12 11 10 09 08
10 9 8 7 6 5 4 3 2 1

New edition ISBN-10:   1-4329-0204-0 (hardcover)
                        1-4329-0213-X (paperback)
New edition ISBN-13:   978-1-4329-0204-9 (hardcover)
                        978-1-4329-0213-1 (paperback)

The Library of Congress has cataloged the first edition as follows:
Oxlade, Chris.
        Trains / Chris Oxlade.
                        p. cm. — (Transportation around the world)
        Includes bibliographical references (p.   ) and index.
ISBN 1-57572-307-7 (library binding)
1.   Railroads — Trains — Juvenile literature.
        [1. Railroads - Trains.] I. Title. II. Series.

TF148 .O95 2001
625.1 — dc21

                                                                00-010065

Acknowledgements
The publishers would like to thank the following for permission to reproduce photographs: Alamy pp. **6** (Martin Bond), **17** (Iain Masterton); R.D. Battersby p. **16**; Steve Benbow p. **14;** Sylvia Cordaiy pp. **7**, **8**, **23**, **27**; Digital Vision p. **24**; Eye Ubiquitous pp. **4**, **11**; Getty Images p. **10** (Stone/Richard A. Cooke, III), **28** (National Geographic/Justin Guariglia); James Davis Travel Photography p. **18**; Milepost p. **25**; PA Photos p. **15**; Pictures p. **13**; QA Photos p. **20**; Quadrant pp. **12**, **21**, **26**; Science Photo Library p. **29**; SNCF p. **19**; Tony Stone Images pp. **5**, **9**; VSOE p. **22.**

Cover photograph reproduced with permission of Getty Images/Taxi (Michael Dunning).

Every effort has been made to contact copyright holders of any material reproduced in this book. Any omissions will be rectified in subsequent printings if notice is given to the publisher.

Contents

Some words are shown in bold, **like this**. You can find out what they mean by looking in the glossary.

What Is a Train?

A train is a machine that moves along on metal rails. Passengers travel inside the train's **cars**. The cars are pulled along by a **locomotive**.

A train can have many cars or just a few.

cars

A train driver sits in a small **cab** at the front of the locomotive. There are handles and pedals to make the train start and stop. They also make the train speed up and slow down.

There are many instruments in the cab to help the driver drive the train.

How Trains Work

wires

locomotive

80

The wires above the track give power to an electric train.

Some trains are **electric** trains. Electric motors in the **locomotive** make its wheels turn, moving the train along. The electricity comes from wires above the track.

This locomotive uses diesel fuel to power the engine.

Some trains have a **diesel** locomotive. It has a huge **engine** called a diesel engine. The engine needs **fuel** to make it work.

Old Trains

barrel

Water was carried in the barrel on the back of this locomotive. The engine heated the water to make steam.

Early trains used **steam** for power. The first steam **locomotive** was called the Rocket. It was built in 1829 and carried passengers between Liverpool and Manchester in England.

This is a large steam locomotive.

Monster steam locomotives had very powerful **engines**. They pulled **freight** trains with hundreds of **cars** of **cargo** across the United States in the 1940s.

Steam Trains

In some countries, trains are still pulled by **steam locomotives**. Inside the locomotive there is a roaring fire. This makes water boil to form steam.

Steam locomotives still carry passengers and **cargo** in some countries.

Trains need enormous engines and wheels to pull heavy cargo long distances.

On a steam locomotive, steam makes **pistons** move in and out. Long rods are attached to the pistons. The rods make the wheels spin around.

Where Trains Are Used

Trains can be used only where there is a track laid for them. Most tracks are made up of two metal rails. Colored lights called signals tell train drivers when to stop or go.

This train can switch from one track to another.

signals

Railway tracks go between towns and cities. They go from station to station. Passenger trains stop at stations to let passengers get on and off.

Passenger trains like this one carry only people and their luggage. They do not carry **cargo**.

Going to Work by Train

Every day millions of people travel to work and school on **commuter** trains. These trains stop at most stations. They pick up passengers and take them into city centers.

Commuter trains often run only during working hours.

Commuter trains have a lot of wide doors so that the passengers can get on and off the train quickly. There are seats inside the **cars**. There is also space for passengers to stand if all the seats are taken.

Railway stations are busy places.

Underground Trains

This underground train is arriving at the station.

Underground trains travel through tunnels deep beneath the busy city streets. The stations they stop at are also under the ground. All underground trains are **electric** trains.

Underground trains avoid the busy traffic above ground. They can get very crowded during the rush hour. Inside the **cars**, there are plenty of handles for standing passengers to hold onto.

In some busy cities, **cars** on underground trains get very crowded.

handles

Express Trains

Express trains travel along at more than 125 miles (200 kilometers) per hour. They carry people quickly between cities. The famous Japanese "bullet train" is an express train.

This bullet train is traveling past Mount Fuji in Japan.

Express trains like this one travel quickly between cities.

The front of an express train has a smooth, **streamlined** shape. The train slices easily through the air. This helps it speed along.

Shuttle Trains

tunnel

This shuttle train travels underneath the English Channel between England and France.

Shuttle trains go back and forth between two stations. Some of the trains carry cars and buses. Others carry trucks.

Shuttle trains are often used as **commuter** trains between two countries.

Passengers drive their cars onto the shuttle at one end of the journey. They can stay in their cars on the train. They drive off again when the train reaches the other end.

Luxury Trains

Some long-distance trains are very **luxurious**. Passengers have their own **cabins** to sleep in overnight. The famous Orient Express is a luxury train.

The Orient Express travels through Europe and Asia.

A meal in a dining car on a luxury train is a special event.

On a luxury train, the passengers eat their meals in a special **car** called a dining car. It is like a restaurant on wheels. Meals are cooked in part of the car called the galley.

Freight Trains

A **freight** train carries **cargo** instead of passengers. The cargo is carried in special **cars**. Each car is connected to the next one with a hook called a coupling.

When freight trains instead of trucks carry cargo, it helps keep the roads less crowded.

Railway tracks are built on a layer of small pieces of rock called ballast. Special freight cars can spread new ballast when it is needed. A hole in the bottom of the car opens to let the ballast out.

ballast

ballast

This train spreads new ballast on the track where it is needed.

Mountain Trains

Mountain trains can go up much steeper hills than other trains. The **engine** of a mountain train must work very hard to climb the mountains. Mountain railways also need special tracks.

This train is climbing up the Alps, a mountain range that goes through France, Italy, and Switzerland.

rack

A mountain train needs a rack
to pull it up the steep track.

Mountain railway tracks have a rack between the rails. A **locomotive** has an extra wheel that fits into the rack. It stops the train from sliding back down the steep track.

Maglev Trains

The name *maglev* is short for *magnetic levitation*. This means "being held in the air by magnets." A maglev train floats just above its track because of magnetic levitation.

Maglev trains can travel as fast as bullet trains.

A trip in a maglev train is very fast and comfortable.

There are very strong magnets in a maglev track and train. They push against each other. This forces the train upward and forward. Maglev trains are fast and quiet.

Timeline

1803 British engineer Richard Trevithick builds the first **steam locomotive**.

1830 The first passenger railway is opened in England between Liverpool and Manchester. The trains are pulled by a steam locomotive called the Rocket.

1863 The world's first underground railway is opened in London, England.

1879 The first **electric** locomotive is demonstrated in Berlin, Germany.

1883 The Orient Express luxury train makes its first journey between Paris, France, and Istanbul, Turkey.

1940s Enormous Big Boy locomotives are built in the United States for pulling **cargo** trucks.

1981 In France, the TGV express train makes its first journey between the cities of Paris and Lyon.

1982 A maglev railway is opened at an airport in England.

2004 Two Spanish companies make train wheels that can change widths. This helps trains run on different types of tracks in different countries.

Glossary

cab   space at the front of a locomotive where the train driver sits

cabin   private room for passengers on a train

cargo   goods that are moved from place to place

car   part of a train that is pulled by a locomotive. It can carry passengers or cargo.

commuter   person who travels to work by car or train

diesel   type of engine that needs fuel to run

electric   using electricity to run

engine   machine that uses fuel to power movement

freight   cargo transported by train or ship

fuel   substance that burns to make heat

locomotive   vehicle with an engine or motor that pulls cars along a railway track

luxurious   very comfortable

piston   rod that moves in and out of a cylinder

steam   water that has become a gas

streamlined   curved and smooth

Find Out More

Hill, Lee Sullivan. *Trains.* Minneapolis, MN: Lerner, 2002.

Shuter, Jane. *Riding the Rails: Rail Travel Past and Present.* Chicago: Raintree, 2004.

Simon, Seymour. *Seymour Simon's Book of Trains.* New York: HarperTrophy, 2004.

Index